Also by Mohammed Musthafa Soukath Ali, available at leading online retailers.

1. Scrum Narrative and PSM Exam Guide.

2. A Pocket Guide to Passing Professional Scrum Master (PSM 1).

3. Get SAFe Now : A Lightning Introduction to the Most Popular Scaling Framework on Agile.

4   A Lightning Introduction to Scrum.

##

The Professional Scrum™ Product Owner

Guide to Pass PSPO™ 1 Certification

First Published Mar, 2016

Rev. 1.2

Revised Jun 10, 2017

##

Table of Contents

##

Why PSPO 1 certificate?

As a leading framework of bringing agility in product development, Scrum continues to prove as an effective new way of working. This new way is rapidly making into many organizations, in particular the software development divisions due to the transformational results it delivers.

The central role in Scrum Team is Product Owner role whose responsibility is to maximize the value of the product and optimize the work of the Development Team. The likelihood of product success will be in jeopardy if the Product Owner doesn't fulfill the role as conceived by Scrum. So, there is increasing need for the Product Owners and those who shape the product, to understand the full dimension of the Product Ownership in its original form and benchmark their learning.

The most meritorious certificate of all that certify Scrum Product Owner, is the Professional Scrum Product Owner (PSPO) by Scrum.org. In addition, here are the reasons to like this certificate. Here is the list:

• PSPO assessment requires good knowledge of original version of Scrum and its passing requirements are high (85%). Such stringent criteria to obtain the certification provides more teeth to its certificate, than the other similar certifications provided in the marketplace.

• It is administered by a company guided by Ken Schwaber, who is one of the founders of Scrum.

• PSPO does not require any mandatory training courses.

• PSPO assesses the knowledge on authentic Scrum and Product Ownership without any new clout.

• Its fee is nominal @ $200.

• After paying the fee, the password for the assessment is usually sent to registered email instantly and the password does not have any expiration date.

• The assessment can be taken from anywhere with a computer and internet connection.

- Once you acquire the certificate, you do not need to renew. It is a certificate for lifetime.

- The name will be added to Scrum.org's list of Professional Scrum Product Owner 1 in their website so anyone can verify your credentials.

- There are no prerequisite qualifications for the assessment.

##

How to register and attend the assessment

- Please check Scrum.org for latest fee. As of writing this book, it is $200.

- If you took a paid training from Scrum.org - Professional Scrum Product Owner™, you will get one free attempt on PSPO. The password for the assessment will be emailed within 3-5 business days. However, taking a training course is not a prerequisite to take the assessment.

- To register for assessment, go to https://www.scrum.org/Assessments/Professional-Scrum-Product-Owner-Assessments. You don't need to login.

- Click on "BUY PSPO I ASSESSMENT" button. It takes you to "Shopping Cart" page. Shopping cart is already pre-filled with quantity as 1. You can proceed to "Check out."

- The next page requires you to provide customer information including billing address. After providing this information, you can proceed to "Continue to payment method."

- In the next page, you need to provide payment information. You can pay by credit card or use paypal.

- If non-USA cards, equivalent amount for 200 US dollars will be deducted by your card issuer subject to their currency conversion rules. Sometimes, you have to call your card issuer (bank) to remove any limits / security settings on your card before paying. You can also clarify with them about the local currency conversion rate that will be applied.

- After paying the fee, the password for the assessment is sent to registered email usually within a business day. In practice, we see that the password is usually mailed to the registered email instantly, even on holidays and weekends.

- The password does not have any expiration date.

- Use Chrome or Firefox browser. Internet Explorer usually works fine too. However, Scrum.org cautions that certain version of Internet Explorer have been shown to be less reliable.

- To attend the assessment, go to https://www.scrum.org/Assessments/Professional-Scrum-Product-Owner-Assessments.

- Click on hyperlink "Start PSPO I Now". It will prompt you to login. Login to Scrum.org account. If you haven't registered yet, please do so now.

- Enter the assessment password.

- You will be shown a page with technical considerations and quiz buttons. Read all the instructions.

- Once you click "Start this Assessment", the quiz is launched and clock starts ticking.

##

I already know Scrum. What additional knowledge is needed?

The rough break-up of knowledge areas tested in PSPO is provided below. The percentages discussed here are neither accurate quantification nor shared by Scrum.org. These are normalized ranges that are based on the feedback that the Author collected from random PSPO takers.

- Scrum Framework and Scrum Theory: 25%

- Product Owner Roles and Responsibilities: 25%

- Product Backlog Management: 15%

- Cross-Functional and Self-Organization: 15%

- Maximizing the Value of the Product and the work of Development Team: 10%

- Product Ownership in scaled Scrum: 5%

- Miscellaneous from Open Assessments in Scrum.org: 5%

For scoring two-third of the exam, it is essential that you should be prepared as much as it is needed to pass PSM 1. It covers Scrum Framework and Scrum Theory, Cross-Functional and Self-Organization, and partial knowledge on Product Owner role and Product Backlog Management. If you have already passed PSM 1 with good score, you can refresh that knowledge and focus on additional preparation for PSPO. This book helps with that additional preparation needed for PSPO.

This book provides required information on following areas in separate sections. Each section has a quiz at the end.

- Product Owner Roles and Responsibilities.

- Product Owner involvement as he/she traverses through Scrum lifecycle.

- Product Backlog Management.

- Maximizing the value of the product and the work of Development Team.

- Product Ownership in scaled Scrum.

##

##

I did not complete PSM 1. Is that knowledge needed?

It is of paramount importance that you need to have sound understanding of Scrum as defined in Scrum Guide. Here are five short sample Scrum tests to test your Scrum knowledge. If you score high in the first test, i.e., a minimum of 9, then you can go to next sample test.

In case, you score less than 9 in a sample Scrum test, analyze what you missed. If it was a due to a minor misunderstanding but you still feel confident on your Scrum knowledge, you can go to next sample test.

After completing all the four sample Scrum tests, if you have scored over 90% on the average, you have reasonable knowledge of Scrum. You can proceed with the rest of the book to augment your preparation for PSPO.

If you scored less than 90% in the Scrum tests above, and if you are going for PSPO directly without PSM 1, it is strongly recommended that you spend time on equipping yourself with the knowledge needed for PSM 1. Another book by the author "Scrum Narrative and PSM Exam Guide" will help you with that. Please mail your purchase order of this book to psm1examguide@gmail.com for a promotional code. You can use the promotional code to purchase a discounted copy of "Scrum Narrative and PSM Exam Guide" book.

##

Scrum Test 1

Scrum Test 1 - Questions

1.   Scrum Team uses the information of Scrum artifacts to make ongoing decisions. The soundness of these decisions depends on

   a)   Artifacts' Adaptability

   b)   Artifacts' Transparency

   c)   Artifacts' Agility

   d)   Artifacts' Format

2.   An organization decides to have very small Development Teams of size fewer than three. The likely result could be

   a)   The team may have decreased interaction

   b)   The team may have skills shortage

   c)   The team may have low productivity gains

   d)   All of the above

3.   The product development project is about delivering an internal feature for an organization. The team has good skill composition and worked in similar projects. The Sprint lengths can be

   a)   decided after the first release

   b)   ignored since it is internal project

   c)   up to one calendar month

4.   Select all that apply. Empiricism provides...

   a)   frequent opportunities to get information using which uncertainty can be completely eliminated

b) frequent opportunities to discuss different possibilities

c) frequent opportunities to make informed decisions, reducing risk

5. The leadership model followed by Scrum Master is

a) Micro Management

b) Servant Leadership

c) Command and Control

6. During a Sprint Review, the stakeholders notice that the product development progress is not very clearly visible and lacked transparency. Moreover, they are not able to understand the next steps. Who is responsible for this?

a) Development Team

b) Product Owner

c) Scrum Master

d) Scrum Team

7. In the middle of a Sprint, a team member was required by another department manager to support an important task outside the Sprint work. What is recommended for the team member to do?

a) The team member must support since it is important task

b) The team member should ask the manager to speak with the Scrum Master

c) The team member should politely decline and explain the manager about his ownership and accountability for the Scrum Team

8. When more Scrum Teams are added to a project that works on one single product, the productivity of the original Scrum Teams mostly likely will increase

a) True

b) False

9. Select all that apply. Within just few Sprints, Scrum increases the transparency of the following

a) Technical ability of team to create Product Increment

b) Information of real progress

c) Both

10. The architectural features of product need to be

a) Evolved along with Sprint deliveries

b) Completely designed upfront before the Sprints

c) Decided at least at skeleton level in Sprint zero

Scrum Test 1 - Answers

1. Correct answer is 'b'. Significant aspects of the development process must be visible to those responsible for outcome. These aspects must be highly transparent (should provide accurate and same understanding) so appropriate decisions can be taken.

2. Correct answer is 'd'. While the Development Team should be small enough to be nimble, fewer than three Development Team members decrease interaction and results in smaller productivity gains. Smaller Development Teams may encounter skill constraints during the Sprint, causing the Development Team to be unable to deliver a potentially releasable Increment.

3. Correct answer is 'c'. Sprint length should be decided for all Sprints including for the first Sprint. Sprints are limited to one calendar month. Product Owner's input need to sought to verify that the business risk due to this Sprint length is acceptable to them.

In this case, since the team is cross-functional and experienced, risk appears to be lower. So it can be shorter.

4.   Correct answers are 'b' and 'c'. Empiricism is alternative to waterfall to manage complexity and uncertainty. In waterfall, risk of uncertainty accumulates over long cycles. The risk is reduced by providing frequent feedback and course correction points, where more information may be available to view different possibilities and make informed decisions. However, empiricism doesn't completely eliminate uncertainty.

5.   Correct answer is 'b'. The Scrum Master is a servant-leader for the Scrum Team.

6.   Correct answer is 'b'. Product Owner is responsible for maintaining the transparency of Product Backlog, the progress so far, and the next steps along with alternatives if any.

7.   Correct answer is 'c'. Other than the "Backlog Refinement", the Development Team should work on the tasks related to Sprint goal. If any external authority brings different work, the team should explain about how they self-organize their work in Scrum way. After that, the team can refer them to speak with the Product Owner if the external authority still wants to add this new work.

8.   Correct answer is 'b'. Each Scrum Team needs to mutually define their definition of "Done" so their combined work will be potentially releasable. This involves some overhead work in syncing up, and hence the impact to productivity.

9.   Correct answer is 'c'. Since a Sprint fully completes one full cycle of development activities including Sprint Planning, developing, delivering a releasable Increment, etc. it brings out lot of useful information and transparency.

10.   Correct answer is 'a'. Some teams may customize the Scrum to include an iteration zero or Sprint zero before first Sprint, to do design. This is replacement of traditional "Big Upfront Design" of waterfall, and defeats the purpose of empiricism.

##

Scrum Test 2

Scrum Test 2 – Questions

1. Definition of "Done" is

   a) Initially defined per product by Scrum Team, but may change throughout the product development duration

   b) Initially defined per Scrum Team, and doesn't change

   c) Defined after first Sprint based on the new insights obtained from first Sprint Review

2. Which of the following statements are true? Select all that apply

   a) After Sprint Planning, a sprint cannot proceed without complete requirement specification

   b) After Sprint Planning, a sprint cannot proceed without a Sprint Goal

   c) After Sprint Planning, a sprint can proceed without complete Sprint Backlog

   d) After Sprint Planning, a sprint cannot proceed without complete architecture

3. A Development Team is self-organized and empowered. It is also the authority on deciding what business needs are required to be developed

   a) True

   b) False

4. Who decides the duration of the Sprint?

   a) Product manager

   b) Scrum Master

   c) Development Team

   d) Scrum Team

5.   A Product Owner is not available for Scrum events and not supportive enough for Development Team. The next immediate accountability is with

   a)   Development Team that needs to cancel the Sprint

   b)   Stakeholders that need to get a written commitment from Product Owner

   c)   Product Owner's manager who needs to engage the Development Team and understand their problems

   d)   Scrum Master, who needs to educate Product Owner on his role

6.   When a Product Backlog is retired?

   a)   When the Product Owner retires

   b)   When all the Sprints are over

   c)   When the Product retires

   d)   When the Customer provides the sign-off on completion of the project

7.   A Product Owner cannot send a representative (delegate) to the Sprint Review.

   a)   True

   b)   False

8.   A Product Owner is also knowledgeable on technology. In addition to product requirements, they also impose some technical conditions that the product should meet. These conditions must be added to

   a)   Product Backlog

   b)   Sprint Backlog

   c)   Definition of "Done"

9.   An increment is

a) The sum of the value of all increments from previous iterations integrated with the Product Backlog Items "done" in latest Sprint

b) The sum of Product Backlog Items selected into Sprit Backlog

c) The sum of Product Backlog Items "done" in latest Sprint

10. What are the true statements?

a) Scrum Team is responsible for formulating a Sprint Goal

b) When existing Product Backlog Items in the Sprint Backlog are modified, the Sprint Goal is bound to become invalid

c) The coherence between Product Backlog items is made transparent by Sprint Goal. Lack of coherence will lead to them working individually

Scrum Test 2 – Answers

1. Correct answer is 'a'.

2. Correct answers are 'b' and 'c'.

3. Correct answer is 'b'.

4. Correct answer is 'd'. The final Sprint duration, i.e., how much shorter than one month, is decided by the Scrum Team after considering the need of the Product Owner to limit business risks and the need of the Development Team so they can synchronize the development work with other business events.

5. Correct answer is 'd'. Scrum Master has the responsibility to remove Development Team's impediment and coach every role. Also, Scrum Master can show the resultant poor results due to lack of Product Ownership to Product Owner during retrospective.

6.   Correct answer is 'c'. A Product Backlog is a living artifact that lives as long the Product lives.

7.   Correct answer is 'a'. A Product Owner though they are accountable for Product Backlog, they can delegate many of the activities around Product Backlog Management, such writing them, ordering them, etc. However, they cannot delegate their participation in Scrum events.

8.   Correct answer is 'c'. Every Product Backlog item should be about the product need that carries business value. The condition that Product Owner brings here is about the technical constraint. So, it should be added to the definition of "Done".

9.   Correct answer is 'a' The Increment is the sum of all the Product Backlog items completed during a Sprint and the value of the increments of all previous Sprints.

10.   The Sprint Goal provides opportunity for team members to work together and offers some flexibility of adjusting the Product Backlog items when required. Development Team can modify the Product Backlog Items in the Sprint Backlog with Product Owner's consent, such that the Sprint Goal will still be met. Correct answers are 'a' and 'c'.

##

Scrum Test 3

Scrum Test 3 - Questions

1. The role of Scrum Master in Sprint Retrospective is

   a) Auditor

   b) Silent Observer

   c) Peer Team Member

   d) None of the above

2. To deliver a single product, three different Development Teams are formed. How many Product Owners are needed?

   a) As many as recommended by Scrum Master

   b) Three

   c) One

3. Scrum framework is founded on

   a) Empiricism

   b) Empiricism and Technical Practices

   c) Empiricism and Emotional Intelligence

4. After Sprint Review, Production release in Scrum requires

   a) Hardening Sprints

   b) Non-Functional Testing

   c) Architectural Validations

   d) Usability/End User testing

e)   All of the above

f)   None of the above

5.   A Scrum Team crafts the following Sprint Goal: "All the Sprint code should have passed 100% automated unit tests".

a)   Not an appropriate goal, since Sprint goal should be about expected business value

b)   It is incorrect, since Product Owner formulates the goal and not the Scrum Team

c)   It is well formed Sprint Goal

6.   One of the Scrum Teams chose to have a Development Team member also playing the role of Scrum Master. A Development Team member cannot also play Scrum Master's role.

a)   True

b)   False

7.   Duration (length) of the Sprint is decided by

a)   Product Owner

b)   Scrum Master

c)   Scrum Team

8.   During Daily Scrum, this plan is used as a reference to understand the changes in progress.

a)   Sprint Backlog

b)   Product Backlog

c)   Sprint Burn-down

9.   An important executive wants the Development Team to take in a highly critical feature in the current Sprint. The Development Team

   a)   Will work on that since organization priority is more important

   b)   Will ask the executive to work with Product Owner

   c)   As empowered team, will seek the executive to select an alternative work to be removed instead

10.   A Scrum Team is in the process of defining Product Backlog items. The Scrum Master notices that the team is not using User Story format to capture the backlog items. Scrum Master should

   a)   correct the team's behavior by coaching them about user stories

   b)   let the team decide the format of Product Backlog items

   c)   add a business analyst with knowledge of writing user stories to the team, with specific responsibility of documenting backlog in terms of user stories

Scrum Test 3 - Answers

1.   Correct answer is 'c'. One of the items reviewed in retrospective is the "implementation of Scrum framework." Since Scrum Master is the owner for that, they participate as a peer team member.

2.   Correct answer is "c." A single product should have a single Product Backlog and hence the only one owner, a Product Owner. A Product Owner can delegate some of his responsibilities to the team; however they are still accountable for Product Backlog ownership.

3.   Correct answer is "a." Technical practices or any other value adding techniques can be optionally chosen by the Team and followed within the Scrum framework. However they don't reflect the foundation of Scrum.

4.   Correct answer is 'f'. Every Sprint produces potentially releasable production quality Increment.

5.   Correct answer is 'a'. Sprint Goal reflects the intended business functionality that will be delivered in a Sprint.

6.   Correct answer is 'b'. A Scrum Master can be a Development Team member but that is not mandatory.

7.   Correct answer is 'c'.

8.   Correct answer is 'a'. The Sprint Backlog is a plan with enough detail that changes in progress can be understood in the Daily Scrum.

9.   Correct answer is 'b'.

10.   Correct answer is 'b'. Scrum doesn't prescribe any specific technique to capture the Product Backlog items. The team can choose the most beneficial technique that works for them.

##

Scrum Test 4

1.   Which is not a Product Backlog Management activity?

  a)   Clearly expressing and ordering Product Backlog items

  b)   Optimizing the value of the work the Development Team performs

  c)   Using formal change control to manage Product Backlog when market provides feedback from Product usage.

  d)   Ensuring the Development Team understands items in the Product Backlog to the level needed.

2.   Select all that apply. Scrum Team participates in

  a)   Sprint Planning

  b)   Daily Scrum

  c)   Sprint Review

  d)   Sprint Retrospective

3.   An inspector finds that a work aspect deviates outside acceptable limits, and that the resulting product will be unacceptable. When will the team adjust this work aspect to minimize the deviation?

  a)   In the next Scrum Event

  b)   As soon as possible

  c)   After the Scrum Master approves the adjustment

4.   A Scrum Team can identify the improvements only during the Sprint Retrospective

  a)   True

b)   False

5.   For the first Sprint, the inputs are the Product Backlog and the Projected Capacity of the Development Team. What are the additional inputs to the subsequent Sprints?

   a)   Defect list from previous Sprint

   b)   Sprint Plan

   c)   Past performance of the Development Team

   d)   Latest Product Increment

6.   When a Sprint is cancelled, the Scrum Team discards all the work and refines a new Product Backlog

   a)   True

   b)   False

7.   At the end of Sprint Planning, the Development Team could not decompose all of the work into units of one day or less. It could decompose the work for only the first few days of the Sprint.

   a)   The Development Team should close the Sprint Planning and start the work

   b)   Since the team is self-organized, they should continue Sprint Planning in the following days before they start the work

   c)   The Scrum Master should coach the team in required skills

8.   What is a key inspect and adapt meeting for the Development Team?

   a)   Project Status Meeting

   b)   Daily Scrum

   c)   Design Sessions

9. What are the true statements?

  a) Only the Product Owner should update the Product Backlog without delegating to anyone

  b) Only the Development should be responsible for estimates of Product Backlog Items

  c) Only the Product Owner should cancel the Sprint. Others can influence the decision to cancel.

  d) Only the Product Owner can change the Sprint Backlog

10. Who defines definition of "Done"?

  a) Development Team

  b) Technical / Domain Experts

  c) Product Owner

  d) Scrum Team

Scrum Test 4 – Answers

1. Correct answer is 'c'. Changes in business requirements, market conditions, or technology may cause changes in the Product Backlog. Product Owner keeps the Product Backlog updated as a living artifact to reflect these changes, without a formal change control process.

2. Correct answers are 'a', 'c', and 'd'. Scrum Team participates in all events except Daily Scrum. Only Development Team participates in that event, because, it organizes, plans, and controls its work without direction or management by Product Owner or Scrum Master. Scrum Master can participate if there is a need to coach or facilitate, until the Development Team can do on its own.

3.   Correct answer is 'b'. The Development Team does not wait for any formal event to make this adjustment; instead make it as soon as possible to minimize further deviation.

4.   Correct answer is 'b'. Sprint Retrospective provides a formal opportunity to focus on inspection and adaptation. However, improvements may be identified and implemented any time.

5.   Correct answers are 'c' and 'd'.

6.   Correct answer is 'b'. The team still conducts Sprint Review to review "Done" Product Backlog items. If part of the work is potentially releasable, the Product Owner typically accepts it. All incomplete Product Backlog Items are re-estimated and put back on the Product Backlog.

7.   Correct answer is 'a'. The Sprint Planning is time boxed and cannot be extended. It is enough to have the work decomposed for first days of the Sprint to start the work, and can be decomposed later as needed throughout the Sprint.

8.   Correct answer is 'b'. Daily Scrums improve communications, eliminate other meetings, identify impediments to development for removal, highlight and promote quick decision-making, and improve the Development Team's level of knowledge. This is a key inspect and adapt meeting for Development Team.

9.   Correct answers are 'b' and 'c'.

10.   Correct answer is 'a'. It is developed by the Development Team with conditions that are acceptable to Product Owner.

Product Owner

------------------------DE-TOUR------------------------

In this chapter, the following are included for clarity and context. They are not part of The Scrum Guide:

Product Owner in contract work, Issues in implementing Product Owner role

------------------------DE-TOUR------------------------

What is expected from Product Owner?

In Scrum, Product Owner is expected to act as the ultimate owner the product. Even the top executive of the company needs to support Product Owner in his/her ownership of the product.

The Product Owner possesses a strong inclination to maximize the value of the product by constant collaboration with stakeholders and defining the product needs. Product Owner keeps the product needs ordered, makes the Scrum Development Team understand the needs, optimizes the Development Team's work, releases the product Increment to use, collects and feeds the insights back into Product refinement. They bring transparency to the above activities by owning and maintaining the Product Backlog artifact.

Product Owner is responsible for maintaining the

• Product Backlog Order by sequencing the items to best achieve goals and missions.

• Product Backlog Content by clearly expressing Product Backlog items and by updating it with latest insights and customer/market needs.

• Product Backlog Availability by ensuring that the Product Backlog is visible, transparent, and clear to all, and shows what the Scrum Team will work on next.

Throughout the development, Product Owner works to increase the transparency of what product features are completed so far and what is the work pipeline for the. They use the Sprint Review to update this to stakeholders and also forecast product completion date.

What could go wrong with implementation of Product Owner role?

It is common for an organization to identify and staff an existing business manager in the Product Owner role. While this is perfectly alright, Product Owner role is significantly more empowered. This role also requires strong inclination towards collaborative style of product development.

• <u>They are the Owners for evolving the product and should be allowed to act accordingly</u>: The Product Owner represents the desires of a committee (organization) in the Product Backlog. The utmost priority of the Product Owner is to maximize the value of the product. Product users are the most important stakeholders. The Product Owner's decisions are visible in the content and ordering of the Product Backlog. For the Product Owner to succeed, the entire organization must respect their decisions. Those wanting to change a Product Backlog item's priority must address the Product Owner. Product Owner is the only point of contact for the stakeholder/customer/sponsor.

• <u>They should be willing to be continuously available to the team</u>: They continually work with the Team to make them understand the product needs and derive the best value out of their work.

• <u>They are the ultimate authority of Team's work and should act accordingly</u>: Product Owner leverages the team's skills to continually shape the product and uncover new knowledge. So, it is essential that the team should only be working on their product needs. The team should not be "switching the context" of their work. Context switching occurs when external authorities direct the Development Team to do "some other" work. So, the Product Owner is the ultimate authority on what the team should work next. No one is allowed to tell the Development Team to work from a different set of requirements, and the Development Team is not allowed to act on what anyone else says. Even the CEO of the organization cannot request the team to work on something else. Anybody wanting to change the priority must address the Product Owner.

Who should play the Product Owner role in contract efforts?

A Product Owner is not necessarily the customer. If the project is a contract work performed by a service organization, a person within the service organization can play the Product Owner role and represent the customer.

Rules

•   They can be Full/part time for a Scrum Team. They usually support as a single Product Owner for more than one Scrum Team in parallel.

•   Product Owner can delegate one or more responsibilities to others in the team. But they are still accountable for product value.

•   It is mandatory for Product Owner to participate in all events except Daily Scrum.

•   No one can change the Product Backlog other than Product Owner. However, Development Team/Scrum Master/stakeholders can recommend the items that could be added to Product Backlog.

•   No one can cancel the Sprint other than Product Owner. But, Development Team/Scrum Master/stakeholders can influence the Product Owner to take that decision.

•   If a stakeholder or customer needs to communicate anything to the team, they should direct such communications through the Product Owner.

Summary

•   The Product Owner is responsible for maximizing the value of the product and the work of the Development Team.

•   The Product Owner is the sole person responsible for managing the Product Backlog. The Product Owner may have the Development Team do some of the Product Backlog management activities. However, the Product Owner remains accountable.

•   No body including the CEO can modify the Product Backlog. Those wanting to change a Product Backlog item's priority must address the Product Owner.

Quiz - Questions

1.   During a Sprint Review, the stakeholders notice that the product development progress is not very clearly visible and lacked transparency. Moreover, they are not able

to understand the team's next steps. Who bears the primary responsibility for this status?

a)   Scrum Team

b)   Scrum Master

c)   Product Owner

d)   Development Team

2.   A Development Team is requested by an important stakeholder to help them with some external task, since it is urgently required by organization board. The team referred them to Product Owner. In this case, the Scrum Master

a)   Should do nothing, since the team's action was correct

b)   Should coach the team to support senior management requirements

c)   Should form a sub team that can take up such external requests

3.   The number one priority of the Product Owner is

a)   Managing the development work

b)   Guarding the Development Team from any interruptions

c)   Maximizing the value of Development Team's work

d)   Testing the Development Team's work against detailed requirements

4.   It is the responsibility of the Scrum Master to engage the stakeholders to maximize the value of the product

a)   True

b)   False

5.   Who makes the decision to fund the next Sprint?

a)   Project Sponsor

b)   Project Management Office (PMO)

c)   Product Owner

d)   Product Manager

6.   A Product Owner

a)   directs the Development Team

b)   controls the Scrum process

c)   guides the business analysts

d)   controls the project

e)   optimizes the value of Development Team's work

7.   Scrum is best described as

a)   Software methodology

b)   Framework for developing and sustaining complex products

c)   Product development process

d)   Collection of best practices

8.   Throughout the effort, who takes the ownership of scrum events, sets-up the meeting for every event, and invites the required participants?

a)   Project Manager

b)   Scrum Master

c)   Scrum Team

9.   What are the roles in a Scrum Team? Select all that apply

a)   Project Manager

b)   Programmer

c) Tester

d) Business Analyst

e) Architect

f) Operations Analyst

g) None of the above

10. A Product Owner cannot send a representative (delegate) to the Sprint Review.

a) True

b) False

11. Choose two true statements

a) Development Team can't act on directions from anyone other than Product Manager

b) Product Owner's decisions are visible in the Sprint Backlog content

c) Product users are the most important stakeholders

d) The utmost priority of the Product Owner is to maximize the value of the product

12. Who is responsible for quality in Scrum?

a) Product Owner

b) Tester

c) Scrum Master

d) Everyone who performs the development work

13. The key stakeholders invited to the Sprint Review

a) provide feedback on the team working style

b) provide feedback on Scrum implementation

c)   provide feedback on the Increment

d)   provide feedback on the technical design

14.   Select all that applies. In Scrum, the person playing the business role, Product Owner

a)   Hands over the Product Backlog to the Development Team and leave the team alone. They only meet up again later during final product delivery

b)   Freezes the Product Backlog and tries not to change them afterwards

c)   Works only with designated people in the Development Team

d)   Continuously collaborates with the Development Team, sometimes almost every day

15.   Same person can play both Scrum Master and Product Owner roles

a)   Yes

b)   No

Quiz - Answers

1.   Entire Scrum Team is responsible for "how they planned and performed their work". So, if there was a question about who is responsible for failure or success of scrum work, the answer is the Scrum Team for sure.

The Scrum Master of course needs to help the Product Owner in coaching the techniques for better backlog management, increasing the transparency of backlog, and more. So, the Scrum Master's responsibility is to coach the team to adhere to Scrum and its principles. However, Scrum Master does not bear the primary responsibility for those items that are clearly owned by specific role.

There are clearly defined responsibilities for each role as well. In this case, the question is - who is responsible for a specific activity of backlog management including its transparency. Following are the guidance from Scrum Guide as to this subject:

- The Product Owner is the sole person responsible for managing the Product Backlog.

- Product Backlog management includes Ensuring that the Product Backlog is visible, transparent, and clear to all, and shows what the Scrum Team will work on next

- The Product Owner is responsible for the Product Backlog, including its content, availability, and ordering

- The Product Owner discusses the Product Backlog as it stands. He or she projects likely completion dates based on progress to date

------

So, for this question, the best choice is the "Product Owner"

Correct answer is 'c'.

2.   No one is allowed to tell the Development Team to work from a different set of requirements, and the Development Team is not allowed to act on what anyone else says. Correct answer 'a'.

3.   Product Owner does not manage or direct the development work during the Sprints. It is the responsibility of Scrum Master to manage external interruptions. While Product Owner may help with testing, they are not responsible for detailed testing. Correct answer is 'c'.

4.   While the Scrum Master is responsible to help with maximizing the value of outside interactions with the Scrum Team, Product Owner is responsible for continually engaging the stakeholders. Correct answer is 'b'.

5. Correct answer is 'c'.

6. A product owner maximizes the value of the product and optimizes the value of Development Team's work. Product manager achieves this by managing the Product Backlog. Correct answer is 'e'.

7. Scrum is a framework within which appropriate processes and techniques can be employed to develop complex products. It is neither a methodology nor a software development process. Correct answer is 'b'.

8. Scrum Team is a self-organized team. They manage and organize how they perform their work, and are collectively the owner of their work. Scrum Team together comes up with shared understanding of when to have these events. By bringing in this self-management and regularity, the team avoids the complexities of meeting arrangement and attendance associated with traditional meetings. Scrum Master may facilitate this only during early period, and coach the team to do it by themselves later. Correct answer is 'c'.

9. There are only three roles in a Scrum Team. Correct answer is 'g'.

10. A Product Owner though they are accountable for Product Backlog, they can delegate many of the activities around Product Backlog Management, such writing them, ordering them, etc. However, they cannot delegate their participation in Scrum events. Correct answer is 'a'.

11. Correct answers are 'c' and 'd'.

12. Though Development Team can contain people with testing skills, there is no separate role or title for them in Scrum. Correct answer is 'd'.

13.   In Sprint Review, presentation of the Increment is intended to elicit feedback and foster collaboration The key stakeholders and the Scrum Team collaborate on what to do next .They review how the marketplace or potential use of the product might have changed and what is the most valuable thing to do next. They also review timeline, budget, potential capabilities, and marketplace for the next anticipated release of the product. Correct answer is 'c'.

14.   The Product Owner continuously evolves the ordered list of everything that may be needed in the product. This list is called Product Backlog. Since this list evolves based on the frequent new insights, it requires Product Owner to continuously work with the team communicating about these changing needs, and also clarify the questions about ongoing work. Correct answer is 'd'.

15.   Considering the primary job of each of these roles - a Product Owner wants to maximize/optimize the value of Development Team's work. It is possible for them to push for "more work" while compromising on definition of "Done" or technical quality requirements. They may also overlook the Development Team's empowerment of deciding for themselves how much work they can select for a Sprint.

In such conflicting situations, a Scrum Master teaches both the Product Owner and the Development Team about their empowerment and balances. So, we can see that there should be situations involving conflict of interest if one person plays both roles.

The issue is not about who will play what role. By doing any of that, are we going to have Scrum or not - is the question.

Think about the fundamentals of Scrum. It is risk reduction framework for building complex products. Scrum team is not just self-sufficient. It is also balanced with respect to responsibilities. The risks and subjectivities associated with traditional one man centric Project, are mitigated by distributing the responsibilities between three roles. Now, what happens if you bring Scrum Master and Product Owner under single hat? You can sense the concentration of responsibilities. It increases risk and reduce self-org. Will it be Scrum? The answer is – Product Owner and Scrum Master are separate roles played by different individuals. Correct answer is 'b'.

##

Product Backlog management

------------------------DE-TOUR------------------------

In this chapter, the following are included for clarity and context. They are not part of The Scrum Guide:

Product Vision, Product Roadmap, Release Plan

------------------------DE-TOUR------------------------

It all starts with Product Vision

Before a product comes into being, the vision gives birth to the product idea. The vision is the answer to the question why a product is being built.

Vision is not mandatory part of Scrum framework. However, vision is treated as very significant driver for a great product, by the founder of Scrum. And the PSPO assessment has more likelihood of having one or two questions on vision.

In Software-in-30-days book, the authors day that "Vision is a partially formed idea of something that functions in certain ways, can be used to do work, changes the world or workplace of its users in certain ways, and creates new value or presence in the world or marketplace that previously didn't exist in that form."

In The-Enterprise-and-Scrum book, the author says that "The vision might be vague at first, stated in market terms rather than product terms. The vision will become clearer as the project moves forward. The Product Owner is responsible to those funding the project to deliver the vision in a manner that maximizes their return on investment (ROI). The vision contains the anticipated ROI, release milestones and associated goals."

The vision is advantageous in following ways:

- It creates a shared understanding and enhances alignment.

- It provides a continued reference for making decisions.

- It provides a continued reference for measuring progress.

Vision is elaborated into Product Backlog

To deliver the vision, the Product Owner elaborates it into a Product Backlog. The Product Backlog is an ordered list of product requirements that, when turned into functionality, will deliver this vision.

The vision helps the Product Owner and Scrum Team to compare the relevance and value of the Product Backlog Item against the vision, and then purge the low value items out of Product Backlog. Vision thus helps to keep the size of Product Backlog manageable from becoming a placeholder of innumerable wish list and desires.

The Product Owner continuously evolves the Product Backlog that contains the ordered list of everything that may be needed in the product. Product Backlog is the single source of requirements and changes for the product.

It is quite important that the Product Backlog is accessible and visible to entire Scrum Team and the stakeholders. A Product Owner creates and maintains the Product Backlog to increase the transparency of product plan, plan releases, and capitalize on unforeseen business opportunities.

Product Backlog can provide a view of Product Roadmap of releases and Milestones

Defining the Product Roadmap and associated Release plans are not part of Scrum. While they are good practices, Scrum doesn't mandate them for following reasons:

• Every product Increment is potentially releasable and usable. By defining a separate release planning activity, Scrum Teams may mistake them for including a "separate stabilization" phase to make the Increment fit for release quality.

• Scrum allows people to navigate complexity by being prepared for volatility. By looking far into future and locking down elaborate release plans, Scrum Teams might shift their behavior to following-a-plan than responding to change.

However, Scrum Teams can follow these good practices when they make sense and ensure that they don't fall into wrong behaviors listed above.

For example, when it makes business sense to provide a short term product roadmap for the market, a Product Backlog can be divided into proposed releases for the short term. The sequential list of these releases provides a view of the product roadmap. However, the roadmap and release plans are not set in stone. The priorities and understanding may change once the Sprints start and the grouping of the Product Backlog items into releases can change accordingly.

Another context where this good practice could help is - when the teams grow and scale beyond nucleus Scrum Teams. When more teams work on the same product, it is prudent to have little more look-ahead planning to provide common technical base for multiple teams. This allows the teams to minimize the amount of technical refactoring needed and retain the product's flexibility to continued extension, scaling, and development. Such a look-ahead planning can include initial set of release goals and what-if analysis. The resultant view of the Product Backlog can provide the view of a reasonable product roadmap to the stakeholders.

Product Backlog is never frozen

Product Backlog never gets frozen (never closed for changes), and is a continuously evolving artifact because the Scrum Team and Product Owner in particular are always looking for the changes and opportunities to maximize the value of the product.

Product Owner has unlimited authority to change the Product Backlog anytime.

Using the ordered features, one can understand what the team will work in future.

Since Product Backlog evolves based on the frequent new insights, it requires Product Owner to continuously work with the team communicating about these changing needs, and also clarify the questions about ongoing work.

When is the Product Backlog created?

While there are good practices to come up with an initial Product Backlog, it is not mandatory to have any minimum criteria for the Product Backlog before first Sprint starts. All that is required for the first Sprint to start is- a staffed Scrum Team and set of business ideas to deliver in first Sprint.

First good practice is- A Scrum Team can initially work outside the Scrum Sprints, to create and refine a just enough Product Backlog to get the Sprint work started. It should be made transparent to stakeholders that this activity does not lead to any opportunity of inspecting a useful outcome. Since this activity does not create any working functionality, this activity should not be incorrectly named as a Sprint. The time taken to arrive at the just enough Product Backlog should be as minimal as possible.

Second practice is- to start the Sprint Planning, and refine enough Product Backlog Items for first Sprint, in the Sprint Planning. The team can craft the Sprint Goal, and then come up with the work plan for initial days of the Sprint.

Once the Sprint is in motion, Product Backlog Items are further refined in Product Backlog refinement sessions during the Sprint, so that there will always be some amount of refined items ahead of future Sprints.

• <u>Estimating Product Backlog Items</u>: The people that will do the work of developing Product Backlog items, i.e., the Development Team only can finalize the estimate. Estimating Product Backlog Items is continuous process, through the ongoing act of Backlog Refinement. This estimation is done by Development Team after Product Owner's input.

• <u>Measuring the value of Product Backlog Items</u>: It is mandatory for Product Owner to assign a value for each Product Backlog Item. However, Scrum does not prescribe any technique to measure the business value of the Product Backlog Items. The Product Owner may use one or more appropriate techniques in the industry to estimate the business value.

• <u>Ordering the Product Backlog Items</u>: The Product Backlog Items must be ordered. However, though it is generally ordered based on relative value of individual items, it is not necessarily a hard rule. It is based on the criteria which are deemed as most appropriate by the Product Owner so as to maximize the collective value of the Product and the Development Team's work. In addition to ordering by their business values, Product Owner can consider other factors like cost, risk, coherence, organization policies, and also can seek the input of the Development Team about the technical dependencies between the Product Backlog Items. The Product Owner shall try to optimize the ordering such that it eventually leads to the product Increment with best overall value that is releasable and useable.

How does the Product Backlog look? Is there a format?

The Product Backlog items together represent all that is needed in the product. The items include features, functions, requirements, enhancements, and fixes that constitute the changes to be made to the product in future releases. Scrum does not mandate any format for Product Backlog Items. However, each item must have a description, order, estimate, and value.

What level of detail should be there?

As part of Backlog Refinement, the items are refined until

- they are transparent enough to clearly understand the details and estimate.

- they are small enough for the Development Team so that they can be "Done" within a Sprint.

When a Product Backlog Items reach this state, they are deemed as "Ready" for selection into the Sprint. However, Scrum does not define a formal definition of "Ready."

During the Backlog Refinement, Product Backlog items are decomposed by analyzing their intent. Each item is added with detail, estimate, and the order. Higher ordered Product Backlog items are usually clearer and more detailed than lower ordered ones. More precise estimates are made based on the greater clarity and increased detail; the lower the order, the less detail.

Who needs to participate in Backlog Refinement sessions?

Product Owner owns the Product Backlog. None can bring any change into the Product Backlog without Product Owner's consent. So, Product Owner is present.

In addition, The Development Team helps in refining the items to a level such that the team can complete the items ("Done") within a Sprint. They do this by analyzing, putting together solutions/design, decomposing, and adding details.

On a need basis, they can invite stakeholders to seek answers to product related questions.

Quiz - Questions

1. A Scrum Team can have an exclusive first Sprint to prepare Product Backlog, which is the sole outcome from that Sprint

   a) True

   b) False

2. While a Product Backlog Item can be re-estimated, reordered, modified, they can never be removed from Product Backlog

   a) True

   b) False

3. Product Owner can invite the stakeholders to the Backlog Refinement sessions

   a) Yes

   b) No

4. A Scrum Team noticed that they needed to create additional artifact such as User Interface mark-ups to better explain a product feature. They should NOT do this since Scrum Teams capture the product needs/features only in Product Backlog

   a) True

   b) False

5. When the teams estimate the Product Backlog Items, they only consider the functional need of that Product Backlog Items to arrive at the size

   a) True

   b) False

6. Agile Product Development recommends

   a) Release planning of fully developed Product

b)   Quarterly releases

c)   Early and Frequent release of usable Increments

7.   Pick the true statements

   a)   Product Backlog increases transparency

   b)   It is essential to look at both Sprint Backlog and the Product Backlog to understand what work is identified for the Product

   c)   Product Backlog only contains the functional requirements of the Product

   d)   Product Backlog exists as long as the Product exists

8.   Product Owner may consider the dependencies on software tools when ordering the Product Backlog

   a)   True

   b)   False

9.   Scrum Team adapts the definition of "Done" during

   a)   Anytime

   b)   Backlog Refinement

   c)   Retrospective

10.   How could the Product Owner reduce the potential waste?

   a)   By deferring the decision to last actionable moment - like not detailing the product needs until they are closer for consideration

   b)   By removing one team member as the team increases productivity

   c)   By working with the Scrum Master and identifying what kind of technical documents are not required

11. For the Product Backlog Refinement act, the Scrum Team needs to define a recurring pre-set time every week outside the current working hours of Development Team.

a) True

b) False

12. Pick correct statement. Before the Sprint Planning

a) Team must have a definition of "Done" formally approved by Product Owner

b) Product Backlog Items must be refined with complete acceptance criteria before they are chosen for Sprint

c) Completed user stories must be posted on the Scrum Board.

d) None of the above

13. Choose two answers. How much refinement is required for a Product Backlog Item?

a) as much as required for the Product Owner and the stakeholders

b) until they are transparent enough to clearly understand the details and estimate

c) they are small enough for the Development Team so that they can be "Done" within a Sprint

d) until every story has detailed acceptance criteria clear enough for testers

e) until the work units require an effort of a day or less

14. Which of the following statements is not correct?

a) Only the people who perform the work can finalize the estimate of Product Backlog Items

b) Product Owner always orders the Product Backlog Items only based on the value of each individual item compared to another item.

c) Multiple Development Teams working for the same product should have only one common Product Backlog

d) A Scrum Master can author a Product Backlog Item for Product Owner's consideration

e) Development Team finalizes the estimate.

15. Pick two answers. Non-functional requirements of the product such as performance, security, etc., can be captured by

a) Writing a separate document capturing the requirements and add as appendix to Product Backlog

b) Adding them to Product Backlog with Product Owner's consent and collaborate to estimate and order them

c) Adding them to definition of "Done" and make the Product Owner aware of them

d) Waiting until the decision of Product Owner to release the Increment. Then, build the non-functional requirements for stabilization

Quiz - Answers

1. A Scrum Team can initially work outside the Scrum Sprints, to create and refine a just enough Product Backlog so that the first Sprint can start after that. However, this initial effort should not be named as a Sprint. Also, it should only take minimal time in terms of few days. Correct answer is 'b'.

2. A Product Backlog Item, if discovered as very low in value and not relevant, needs to be removed. Purging the unnecessary items actually helps to reduce the complexity of Product Backlog. Also, the "done" items are continuously removed as well. Correct answer is 'b'.

3. Stakeholders can be invited to Refinement sessions as needed. Correct answer is 'a'.

4.   While the Product Backlog articulates all that is needed for a product, Scrum Teams can create additional artifacts to explain Product Backlog items if such things add value. Correct answer is 'b'.

5.   A team considers both functional and non-functional needs of the Product Backlog Items to estimate its size. The non-functional needs are typically expressed by definition of "Done". They also consider any dependencies and integration required between the items. Correct answer is 'b'.

6.   Early and Frequent release provides more opportunities for valuable feedback. Quarterly release cycle is a good practice but not mandated by Scrum. Scrum encourages much shorter releases. Correct answer is 'c'.

7.   It is enough to look at Product Backlog to understand what is identified for the product. A Product Backlog can contain initiatives, functional and non-functional needs, enhancements, fixes, ideas, and any other product needs. Correct answers are 'a' and 'd'.

8.   Product Owner may consider the dependencies between Product Backlog Items, not the Development Team's dependencies on software tools they use. Correct answer is 'b'.

9.   Sprint Retrospective is a formal opportunity to adapt the development practices and quality goals. Correct answer is 'c'.

10.   Describing all the Product Backlog Items in full detail early could lead potential waste. Correct answer is 'a'.

11.   This is an ongoing act that happens within the hours of current Sprint, for refining the Product Backlog for upcoming Sprints. The time can be mutually discussed and agreed by Product Owner and the Development Team. Usually it does not take more than 10% capacity of Development Team. There is no separate event outside the Sprint like Sprint zero for Backlog Refinement. Correct answer is 'b'.

12.   Definition of "Done" doesn't need Product Owner approval. User stories and acceptance criteria are good practices but not mandatory part of Scrum. Correct answer is 'd'.

13.   A Product Backlog Item must be decomposed to 'Ready' state where it becomes small enough to be "done" within a Sprint. Correct answers are 'b' and 'c'.

14.   The Product Owner is the ultimate authority of finalizing what needs to be added to Product Backlog Items. However, they can have others provide them with suggestions. So, a Scrum Master can always author an item for Product Owner's considerations. Product Owner strives to maximize the collective value of the Product and the Development Team's work. To achieve that, they can choose to follow any appropriate logic for ordering. It need not always be the individual business value. Correct answer is 'b'.

15.   Correct answers are 'b' and 'c'.

##

Product Owner's involvement in Scrum life cycle

•   Heart of Scrum's execution is a short few week event called Sprint. Each Sprint is like a mini project where set of business needs are converted into a working functionality.

•   Each Sprint has a definition of what is to be built, a design and flexible plan that will guide building it, the work, and the resultant product.

•   These Sprints are iterated so that the Product functionalities are cumulatively built.

•   Iterating the Sprints produce usable functionality through which feedback can be obtained. Continuous flow of feedback through these iterations gradually reduces the risk and increases the value. That's why Scrum is equated to a discovery journey.

Here is a rough sequence of activities in a Scrum Journey, and the involvement of Product Owner at every stage.

Just enough preparation to start the Sprint

1   Sprint starts with a staffed Scrum Team that is constant. Unlike traditional approach of bringing people to work, Scrum brings work to the people. It is staffed with a constant team to avoid staffing complexities.

2   Unlike traditional approach of upfront complete requirements specification, Scrum Team starts first Sprint with just enough Product Backlog. There are no pre-conditions to first Sprint. Availability of a Scrum Team and list of business ideas for first Sprint are enough to start the Sprint.

3   The Product Backlog is an ordered list of everything that might be needed in the product and is the single source of requirements for any changes to be made to the product.

Sprint starts with Sprint Planning Event

4	The input to Sprint Planning is the Product Backlog, the latest product Increment if any, projected capacity of the Development Team during the Sprint, and past performance of the Development Team if available.

5	In Sprint Planning, the plan for the Sprint work is created by the collaborative work of the entire Scrum Team.

6	Sprint Planning is time-boxed to a maximum of eight hours for a one-month Sprint. For shorter Sprints, the event is usually shorter.

7	In Topic one, the Development Team works to forecast the functionality that can be done this Sprint.

8	The number of items selected from the Product Backlog for the Sprint is solely up to the Development Team.

9	After the forecast, the Scrum Team crafts a Sprint Goal.

10	The Sprint Goal is an objective that will be met within the Sprint through the implementation of the Product Backlog.

11	In Topic Two, the Development Team decides how it will build this functionality into a "Done" product Increment.

12	The Product Backlog items selected for this Sprint plus the plan for delivering them is called the Sprint Backlog.

13	Work planned for the first days of the Sprint is decomposed by the end of this meeting, often to units of one day or less.

14	The Development Team self-organizes to undertake the work in the Sprint Backlog.

The outcome of Sprint Planning is Sprint Backlog

15	The Sprint Backlog is a forecast by the Development Team about what functionality will be in the next Increment and the work needed to deliver that functionality.

16	The Sprint Backlog is a plan with enough detail that changes in progress can be understood in the Daily Scrum.

17   Only the Development Team can change its Sprint Backlog during a Sprint.

Sprint Planning also produces Sprint Goal

18   The Sprint Goal can be one coherent business function or any other coherence that causes the Development Team to work together rather than on separate initiatives.

19   Sprint Goal also provides some flexibility to Development Team regarding the Product Backlog Items.

Development Team performs the Development Work

20   At the end of Sprint Planning, the Development Team starts the development work.

21   The team discusses the work item in the Sprint Backlog, and collaboratively decides who will work on what task.

22   Though they may work individually on an item, there is no sole ownership of a Sprint backlog item by an individual team member. This is to ensure that there is increased transparency of work within the team, without any individual boundary.

23   Development work may include necessary product engineering practices. The Development Team is expected to be cross functional enough to have all the skills needed for engineering the product Increment out without any external help.

24   A Product Backlog Item is considered to be completely done, only if it meets the conditions defined in definition of "Done".

Development Team reviews the progress in Daily Scrum

25   The Daily Scrum is a 15-minute time-boxed event for the Development Team to synchronize activities and create a plan for the next 24 hours.

26   Daily Scrum is held at the same time and same place each day to reduce complexity.

27   Only Development Team members participate in the Daily Scrum.

28   The Development Team inspects the progress toward the Sprint Goal and the trend toward completing Sprint Backlog.

29   The Daily Scrum optimizes the probability that the Development Team will meet the Sprint Goal.

30   This is a key inspect and adapt meeting - Daily Scrums improve communications, eliminate other meetings, identify impediments to development for removal, highlight and promote quick decision-making, and improve the Development Team's level of knowledge.

Development Team adjusts the Sprint Backlog as more is learned

31   The Development Team modifies the Sprint Backlog throughout the Sprint, and the Sprint Backlog emerges during the Sprint.

32   During the Sprint, Scope may be clarified and re-negotiated between the Product Owner and Development Team as more is learned.

33   As new work is required, the Development Team adds it to the Sprint Backlog. As work is performed or completed, the estimated remaining work is updated.

Sprint Goal is preserved

34   No changes are made to Sprint Backlog that would endanger the Sprint Goal, Quality goals do not decrease.

35   A Sprint would be cancelled if the Sprint Goal becomes obsolete.

36   Only the Product Owner has the authority to cancel the Sprint, although they may do so under influence of others.

37   When a Sprint is cancelled, the Product Owner typically accepts part of the completed work that is potentially releasable. All incomplete Product Backlog Items are re-estimated and put back on the Product Backlog.

At end of Development Work, the team creates an Increment

38   Increment is the end result of work completed.

39   The Increment is not just the outcome of latest Sprint. It is the sum of all the Product Backlog items completed during a Sprint and the value of the increments from the previous Sprints.

Stakeholders and Scrum Team collaborate in Sprint Review

40   A Sprint Review is held at the end of the Sprint to inspect the Increment. Product Backlog is adapted if needed.

41   This is a four-hour time-boxed meeting for one-month Sprints. For shorter Sprints, the event is usually shorter.

42   This is an informal meeting to elicit feedback and foster collaboration.

43   Scrum Team and key stakeholders participate and collaborate. Product owner takes lead in the product inspections by inviting stakeholders to understand marketplace and sharing current state of product backlog.

44   The Development Team demonstrates the work that it has "Done."

45   The Product Owner projects likely completion dates.

46   They review the timeline, budget, and potential capabilities and marketplace for new Product.

The team together with stakeholders identify the most valuable thing to do next

47   The entire group collaborates on what to do next, a valuable input to subsequent Sprint Planning.

48   The result of the Sprint Review is a revised/adjusted Product Backlog.

Sprint ends with Sprint Retrospective

49   Sprint Retrospective is a formal opportunity where Scrum Team inspects itself and creates a plan for improvements for next Sprint.

50   This is a three-hour time-boxed meeting for one-month Sprints. For shorter Sprints, the event is usually shorter.

51   The Scrum Master encourages the Scrum Team to improve its development process and practices.

52   Scrum Team plans ways to increase product quality by adapting the definition of "Done."

53   The outcome is the list of identified improvements that will be implemented in the next Sprint.

Starting next Sprint

54   Next Sprint starts as soon as the previous Sprint is over. Again, the pre-conditions for starting a Sprint is - the availability of Scrum Team and business ideas for potential Sprint.

Closing the Scrum

55   In Scrum, it is Product Owner's call to decide the closure of the journey. Others can influence this decision.

56   The Product Backlog lives as long as the product lives. So, in theory, you will have the Scrum Team as long as the Product Backlog lives.

Quiz - Questions

1.   The model of taking a small step to produce an outcome, observe the result, and then adjusting next step based on this observation and experience is known as

   a)   empiricism

   b)   predictive analysis

   c)   lean

2.	The Scrum Team gathers for Sprint Planning meeting. The Product Owner has some stories but the team finds that stories do not provide enough information to make forecast. The immediate next best thing to do is

a)	The Scrum Master cancels the Sprint

b)	The Development Team proceeds with starting with whatever is known

c)	The Development Team makes it transparent that they cannot make a forecast with insufficient information, and negotiates with Product Owner on refining the stories to ready state

d)	The Scrum Team discusses the root cause in the retrospective

3.	Under this topic of the Sprint Planning, the Development Team is more active in planning and Product Owner is mostly observing or clarifying

a)	Topic One (What)

b)	Topic Two (How)

c)	Topic Three

4.	By not having a Sprint Goal, a Scrum Team looses the opportunity to summarize the core ------ they are going to solve

a)	Backlog problem

b)	Business problem

c)	Application problem

5.	Throughout the Sprint, Development Team tracks the remaining work and the trend. At a minimum, the remaining work must be updated

a)	Every day

b)	Every Week

c)	Whenever the Scrum Master gets the time

6.   Who makes the decision to fund the next Sprint?

   a)   Project Sponsor

   b)   Project Management Office (PMO)

   c)   Product Owner

   d)   Product Manager

7.   Fill in the blanks. _____ creates the Sprint Goal _____ the Sprint Planning

   a)   Product Owner, during

   b)   Development Team, after

   c)   Product Owner, before

   d)   Scrum Team, during

8.   In the middle of the Sprint, Development Team finds that few more days of work is needed to complete the scope. The planning options include:

   a)   Add more team members

   b)   Catch up using weekends

   c)   Defer the activities like testing after stakeholder's demo

   d)   Involve the Product Owner and negotiate alternatives

   e)   All of the above

9.   Development Team is self-organizing team. It means

   a)   it guards the Scrum implementation

   b)   it manages the Product Backlog

   c)   it manages how to perform the work

10.   After Sprint Planning, Product Owner finds that it makes sense to develop a new functionality.

    a)   Development Team will add that to the Sprint Backlog

    b)   Development Team can review that for selection in the next Sprint.

    c)   Development Team can swap an existing functionality for the new functionality

11.   During the Sprint Review, Scrum Master notices that the Product Owner is not using Product Burn-Down graph to explain the forecast. What should he do?

    a)   Let the event complete this time, but Scrum Master should educate the Product Owner that they must use one of the projection techniques like Gantt chart, Cumulative Flows Burn-down, etc.

    b)   Cancel the event and wait until the Product Owner has created Burn-Down graph

    c)   Do Nothing

12.   A Scrum Team is at the end of a Sprint. The next Sprint starts

    a)   Only after the product Increment is released to production

    b)   Only after the Retrospective event of the current Sprint

    c)   Only after the team for next Sprint is on boarded

    d)   Only after the Sprint Planning

13.   A Development Team decides to divide Sprint Backlog and assign ownership of every Sprint Backlog item to separate individual in the team. The Scrum Master

    a)   Should encourage this practice as it increases productivity

    b)   Should encourage this practice as it increases individual accountability

    c)   Should coach the team to collectively take ownership of Sprint Backlog items though an individual works on an exclusive item

14. In a Retrospective, a Scrum Team decides to revise the Sprint length. Pick three true statements about Sprint length.

a) Sprint length can extend as long as required to complete all the work identified in Sprint Backlog

b) It is better to have Sprints of consistent length through the Scrum journey

c) The new Sprint length needs to be agreed by Product Owner

d) Sprint can have a maximum duration of one month

15. The only time when a Scrum Team can meet stakeholders is Sprint Review

a) Yes

b) No

16. A Development Team gets into a situation in which a conflicting team member's behavior causes issues to the progress. Who is responsible for removing this issue?

a) Management

b) Product Owner

c) Scrum Master

d) Development Team

17. The frequency of updating the Product Backlog is

a) Daily

b) Every Sprint beginning

c) It could be updated any time

d) Anytime using an approved change request

18.   A Development Team is requested by an important stakeholder to help them with some external task, since it is urgently required by organization board. The team referred them to Product Owner. In this case, the Scrum Master

a)   Should do nothing, since the team's action was correct

b)   Should coach the team to support senior management requirements

c)   Should form a sub team that can take up such external requests

19.   In the middle of the Sprint, a Development Team finds that they have more room for additional work. They decide to change the Sprint Backlog by adding few more backlog items from the Product Backlog. Who should be present to decide the additional work and accordingly modify the Sprint Backlog?

a)   Senior members of the Development Team

b)   Scrum Master

c)   Entire Development Team

d)   Product Owner

e)   Scrum Team

20.   This is used by the Product Owner to identify unfinished work at the end of the Sprint

a)   Coding Standard

b)   Definition of Ready

c)   Testing Standard

d)   Definition of "Done"

21.   Which is true statement?

a)   Retrospective focuses on Scrum Team's process and people aspects while Sprint Review focuses on product

b)   Retrospective focuses on product while Sprint Review focuses on Scrum Team's process

c)   Retrospective focuses on Scrum Team's process and people aspects while Sprint Review focuses on Velocity

22.   Scrum Team creates the Sprint Goal. The Product Owner

a)   describes the business objective to the Scrum Team. Based on this and the functionality forecast for the Sprint, the Sprint Goal is crafted

b)   gets the stakeholder's consent for the Sprint Goal

c)   can change the Sprint Goal anytime during the Sprint, and can direct the Development Team to resume the work on the new Sprint Goal.

23.   During the Sprint, while the Sprint Backlog can be modified as more is learned, no changes are made that would endanger the Sprint Goal.

a)   True

b)   False

24.   A Scrum Team is at the end of a Sprint. The next Sprint starts

a)   Only after the product Increment is released to production

b)   Only after the Retrospective event of the current Sprint

c)   Only after the team for next Sprint is on boarded

d)   Only after the Sprint Planning

25.   When does the team create Sprint Backlog?

a)   during the review with stakeholders

b)   along with creation of Product Backlog

c)   during the Sprint Planning

d)   after the Product Backlog Refinement

26.   What activities and events happen between current Sprint end and subsequent Sprint beginning?

a)   No such activities

b)   performance assessment of the team

c)   management retrospective

d)   Product Planning

27.   The Sprint Goal provides the following

a)   Guidance to the team on why it is building Increment

b)   Flexibility to the team about the functionalities implemented in this Sprint

c)   Common but specific goal so that team members can work together

d)   All the above

28.   The outcome from a typical Sprint is

a)   Product Increment with bugs but in working condition to perform the demonstration

b)   Appropriate documents for the review by stakeholders and technical experts

c)   A "Done" working Increment

d)   Estimate for the full development based on the spike work

29.   This shows the trend of remaining effort in the Product Backlog at the end of Sprints.

a)   Burn-up

b)   Burn-down

c)   Burn-trend

30.   Select all that apply. Before starting the first Sprint, what needs to be ensured?

a)   A complete Product Backlog capturing detailed product needs

b)   Availability of Project Manager

c)   Just enough Product Backlog Items with business ideas for first Sprint

d)   Completed System Architecture

e)   Staffed Scrum Team

Quiz - Answers

1.   Empiricism advocates observation rather than prediction to navigate complex adaptive problems. Scrum is founded on empiricism. Correct answer is 'a'.

2.   For the Sprint to begin, there are no pre-conditions except a Scrum Team and a Product Backlog with enough business ideas for the Sprint. It is good practice to have sufficient number of Product Backlog items "Ready" to be selected for the Sprint. If Product Backlog is not clear at Sprint Planning, the Development Team will have difficulty creating a forecast of the Sprint work. The team needs to make it transparent and works with Product Owner to refine them within the Sprint Planning. As soon as possible, Scrum Master can also coach the Product Owner on improving this, for example by having regular "backlog refinement sessions." Answer 'd' is also correct, but the question asks about the "immediate next" step. Correct answer is 'c.'

3.   In topic two, the Development Team puts together a plan of how to achieve the scope of the Sprint. It primarily involves deriving work tasks. As an owner who is going to own and perform these tasks, this team is more active during topic two. Correct answer is 'b'.

4.   Sprint Goal provides an opportunity to understand the summary of the core business goal and how the individual Product Backlog Items selected for the Sprint are connected through this common goal. Correct answer is 'b'.

5.   Scrum requires that remaining work for a Sprint is summed and known on a daily basis. Correct answer is 'a'.

6.   Correct answer is 'c'.

7.   Scrum Team creates the Sprint Goal during the Sprint Planning. Correct answer is 'd'.

8.   Scrum events are time boxed. Sprint needs to be over by defined date. However, the scope of the Sprint may expand or contract as more is learned throughout the Sprint. When new issues emerge that threaten the completion of Sprint by pre-set date-

As a first step, the team needs to capture this as an issue and try to solve on their own. If they cannot, they should make this impediment transparent and take Scrum Master's help. Even after that, if the impediment is not solved, they need to involve the Product Owner to discuss the alternatives and adjust the Sprint work. When the Product Backlog Items originally selected for the Sprint are adjusted, both the Product Owner and the Development Team must be present. Correct answer is 'd'.

9.   Development Team is self-organized in that sense that it chooses to organize how to accomplish its work without any external directions. Correct answer is 'c'.

10.   Product Owner can't introduce the new functionality in the middle of the Sprint unless the Development Team gets more capacity to work and they mutually agree to take this in. After Product Owner adding the new functionality and ordering it to be on

the top of the Product Backlog, the Development can review that for selection in next Sprint Planning. Correct answer is 'b'.

11.   Various projective practices upon trending have been used to forecast progress, like burn-downs, burn-ups, or cumulative flows. These have proven useful. However, these do not replace the importance of empiricism. A Product Owner may want to use these practice if they add value. But they are not mandatory. Correct answer is 'c'.

12.   The Product Owner may choose to release to production but not mandatory. The same team will continue to next Sprint. Sprint Planning is the first event of the Sprint. Next Sprint starts immediately after the current Sprint end, i.e., the Retrospective. Correct answer is 'b'.

13.   The Sprint Backlog is collectively owned by the Development Team. Development Team mutually monitors the work and ensures that the team as a whole complete all the work. Correct answer is 'c'.

14.   The Product Owner needs to ensure that it is short enough to limit business risks and also short enough so the team can synchronize the development work with other business events. Please note that the finalized Sprint length cannot be longer than 1 calendar month. Correct answers are 'b', 'c', and 'd'.

15.   Scrum Team can meet the stakeholders during Backlog Refinement sessions. Correct answer is 'b'.

16.   Think about who is responsible for identifying and removing different types of issues. The Scrum Master is responsible for removing impediments outside Development Team's influence. Also, they are responsible for causing change that increases the productivity of the Scrum Team.

In this case, the issue faced by the Development Team is well within the influence of the Development Team to resolve. So, the Scrum Master should coach the team to resolve this themselves. If the Scrum Master actively takes steps such as removing this person from the Team, in the long term, it will lead to a diminished inclination of the Development Team to resolve internal problems for themselves. Correct answer is 'd'.

17.   Product Backlog is a living artifact and reflects the latest plan for the product. The plan is continuously updated as the product is used and gains value, and the marketplace provides feedback. Correct answer is 'c'.

18.   No one is allowed to tell the Development Team to work from a different set of requirements outside the Product Backlog, and the Development Team is not allowed to act on what anyone else says. Everything that the Development Team works must originate from the Product Backlog. Correct answer 'a'.

19.   Nobody can change the Sprint Backlog other than the Development Team. So Development Team should be present. Product Owner is responsible for optimizing the value of the Development Team's work and is needed to explain the content of the Product Backlog, and give mutual consent on the next work. So the Product Owner also needs to be present. Correct answers are 'c' and 'd'

20.   Definition of "Done" provides the same shared understanding and transparency of what has been done at the end of the Sprint. Correct answer is 'd'.

21.   Retrospective focuses on Scrum Team's process, quality standards like definition of "Done" and People aspects. Correct answer is 'a'.

22.   Sprint Goal doesn't need stakeholders' approval. If the Sprint Goal becomes obsolete, Product Owner must cancel the Sprint. Correct answer is 'a'.

23.   If the Sprint Goal is endangered, it will lead to cancelation of the Sprint. Correct answer is 'a'.

24.   The Product Owner may choose to release to production but not mandatory. The same team will continue to next Sprint. Sprint Planning is the first event of the Sprint. Correct answer is 'b'.

25.   Correct answer is 'c'.

26.   A subsequent Sprint starts immediately after the current Sprint. Correct answer is 'a'.

27.   The Sprint Goal provides guidance to the Development Team. It also provides some flexibility regarding the functionality implemented within the Sprint. The selected Product Backlog items deliver one coherent function, which can be the Sprint Goal. The Sprint Goal can be any other coherence that causes the Development Team to work together common but specific goal. The correct answer is 'd.'

28.   In every Sprint, the Development Team creates at least one piece of functionality that is an Increment of potentially releasable product. The correct answer is 'c'.

29.   Burn-down is a trend line connecting data points of remaining effort of Product Backlog at the end of each completed Sprint. By extending the burn-down line to the x-axis, we can forecast when the project is likely to finish—assuming effort and velocity stay stable. Correct answer is 'b'.

30.	There are no pre-conditions to first Sprint. Availability of a Scrum Team and list of business ideas for first Sprint are enough to start the Sprint. Correct answers are 'c' and 'e'.

##

Maximizing value

-------------------------DE-TOUR-------------------------

In this chapter, the following are included for clarity and context. They are not part of The Scrum Guide:

Return on Investment, Total Cost of Ownership, Validated Learning, Value Measurements

-------------------------DE-TOUR-------------------------

What is value?

Scrum clearly puts the "value" as number one focus for the Scrum Team. However, it neither defines what is deemed as value nor explains how to measure it.

There could be questions around these aspects though. Let's understand them using other literature.

The authors of Software-in-30-days book define that "Value is the measure of how valuable the delivered functionality is to the organization. It is a measure of the effectiveness (a percentage) of each dollar spent on software development that creates value for the organization."

In other words, value involves getting more Return on Investment (ROI) at less Total Cost of Ownership (TCO). Return on Investment is not just about revenue. It could mean different things to different organizations.

What is Return on Investment (ROI)?

Return on Investment refers to favorable benefits for the organization from the product over and above the effort required for building, maintaining, and servicing the product. The benefits are generated by more market and user acceptance of the product. Prioritizing the investment (items on the Product Backlog) on building highly usable features provides the highest chance of creating value and hence ROI.

For the Product Owner, the value for the users and the organization is more important than anything else, because they provide high ROI. Though there is no finite list, some of the aspects such as 'Meeting the functional expectation', 'Ability to be robust and reliable', Ease of Use, etc are typically perceived as value from user point of view.

What is Total Cost of Ownership (TCO)?

TCO includes not just the Product development costs, but also the cost of maintenance, and operations of the product throughout its life. The authors of the book Software-in-30-days classify the cost as capital cost and expenses. Development costs are separated because they can be capitalized. Maintenance and operations costs are expensed.

From the Developer standpoint, aspects such as simplicity (no unnecessary code for example), support documentation, automated test beds, conformance to design and development standards, minimal external dependencies, etc. are typically perceived as means to increase the technical quality. A product with high technical quality reduces the cost of maintenance, and operations of the product throughout its life, leading to lower TCO for the organization.

So, in addition to prioritizing the investment on building highly usable features, Product Owner can have the Development Team optimize the value further by developing a high technical quality product.

Increasing actual ROI and Reducing TCO through Validated Learning

Product Owner is responsible for maximizing the value of the Product and Developer Team work, by ensuring that the outcome has more ROI and less TCO. But the specific process / method / techniques of achieving this value may vary between different organizations.

The prediction of ROI of a product often turns out to be different. Initial assumptions about the product's appeal to users and market acceptance could be proven wrong when the product is finally released to use.

A great way to optimize the actual ROI and reduce the TCO is to build only most valuable features and create increments based on validated learning.

Learning becomes validated learning when the assumptions and plans can be compared with the results. For validated learning, it is essential to release the increment to market and users to learn about the validity of assumptions and plans.

By deferring the low value features and their supporting infrastructure, one can avoid the unnecessary maintenance, reducing TCO.

Reducing Total Cost of Ownership by reducing Technical Debt

Technical debt refers to undone work. When a Development Team makes poor design decisions or sets a diluted definition of "Done" or not meeting the required definition of "Done", it creates quality gaps in the product. These quality gaps create the technical debt that leads to poor quality consequences and decrease the Product value.

The practice that can be used by the Development Team to develop high technical quality Increment is an appropriate definition of "Done". A Development Team follows the common definition of "Done" created by the Development Organization. If an existing definition is not available, the Development Team creates it.

The team must verify the "done" more often during the Sprint to avoid surprises at Sprint end. Scrum does this to ensure that the quality is built into the product from the beginning.

If multiple teams are working on the same product, the definition is not just applied just for a Scrum team's increment but for the integrated product.

Should the Product Owner approve the definition of "Done"?

The Development Team defines the definition of "Done". It is essential for the entire Scrum Team including Product Owner to be well aware of the definition. However, there is no need for approval from Product Owner.

While a Product Owner needs to be involved and made understood about the conditions, it is the Development Team's responsibility to define the conditions in a verifiable way, because many of these conditions are usually around technical quality. For example, Product Owner may want a condition such as "The Increment should be thoroughly tested because it will be released to production", and Development Team may define it such as "The Increment should pass all the automated unit tests with 95% code coverage."

Going beyond ROI and TCO to measure value and success of software

We saw that value involves getting more Return on Investment (ROI) at less Total Cost of Ownership (TCO). However, lately, more balanced measures of value are also being introduced by experts. Such measures go beyond just the ROI and TCO but also look at many others measures to benchmark the success.

Traditionally, projects tend to measure the success in terms of meeting a pre-defined plan. That is, if the project achieves a pre-defined scope of work at acceptable quality, within the pre-defined cost and time, it is deemed as success. Unfortunately, these measures do not necessarily represent elements of value. Though projects may deliver on time, the outcome might be obsolete, the user adoption might be poor, technical quality might make the product very rigid to enhance, etc.

Scrum.org has provided a framework to measure the value of software. It is called Evidence Based Management or EbMgt. EBMgt measure three Key Value Areas (KVA) to measure the value of software:

1.   Current Value

2.   Time to Market

3.   Ability to Innovate

Eleven Key Value Measures are defined under these three KVA.

Current Value:

1.   Revenue Per Employee measures - Gross Revenue /number of employees.

2.   Product Cost Ratio measures - All expenses in the organization that develops, sustains, provides services, markets, sells, and administers the product or system.

3.   Employee Satisfaction measures - Engaged employees that know how to maintain, sustain and enhance the software systems and products are one of the most significant assets of an organization.

4.   Customer Satisfaction measures - Sound management, solid software, and creative, fulfilled employees.

Time to Market:

5.   Release Frequency measures - The time needed to satisfy the customer with new, competitive products.

6.   Release Stabilization measures - The impact of poor development practices and underlying design and code base. Stabilization is a drag on competition that grows with time.

7.   Cycle Time measures - The time (including stabilization) to satisfy a key set of customers or to respond to a market opportunity competitively.

Ability to Innovate:

8.   Installed Version Index - The difficulty customers face installing a new release. The relatively low value of new releases, or even the number of customers that are evaluating alternatives.

9.   Usage Index - Determines a product that is burdensome and difficult to use and excess software that must be sustained even though it is rarely used.

10.   Innovation Rate measures - Growth of technical debt caused by poorly designed and developed software. Budget is progressively consumed keeping the old software alive.

11.   Defects measures - increasingly poor quality software, leading to greater resource and budget to maintain it and potential loss of customers.

Each of these metrics is measured continuously. The continuous array of data provides insight into the trends and patterns. An organization can make changes in the processes, behavior, tooling, etc. and trace their impact on improving these metrics. All these can be consolidated into an overall Agility Index for the organization. Agility Index is an indication of how effective the organization is in delivering value.

Another method for measuring the success and value of the product is recommended by Roman Pichler. It is known as Product Scorecard that has four elements to measure: Financial, Customer, Product & Process, and People.

You as Product Owner can see that there is no hard and fast rule about how to measure the value and success of the product. In fact, a Product Owner chooses the measures that make sense for their context, and then inspects their effectiveness and adapts.

However, there are few things that a Product Owner needs to avoid:

• Avoid the vanity metrics. Vanity metrics are those that seem to provide some surface level quantification but don't necessarily add value.

• Avoid measuring too many aspects. Limit to handful of metrics that are closer and effective reflections of product value and success.

How could the Product Owner measure user feedback?

One of the very significant value measures that many methods discuss is- the user feedback about the product. Eric Ries in his book The-Lean-Startup lists techniques such as A/B split tests, real-time monitoring, funnel analysis, cohort analysis, search engine marketing, etc as some of the techniques that can be used to measure the feedback in a lean startup approach to product building.

Eric is also a proponent of using Net Promoter Score (NPS) to measure the customer satisfaction. While product development in empirical environment requires continuous end-customer feedback, the logistics and practical considerations would limit the frequency of reaching out to end-customer to know their satisfaction. A thumb rule is to collect customer satisfaction every quarterly using intrusive means, meaning that customer will be asked about the satisfaction through the questions. Longer than a quarter may be too long a time to realize that a problem is brewing, and shorter than quarter may be too frequent to disturb the customer with surveys and questions.

Quiz – Questions

1. Which one has the highest chance of creating value for Organization?

   a) Spending on maintaining and sustaining products and systems

   b) Spending on building highly usable features of the Product

   c) Spending on building all of the desirable features of the Product

2.   How the Product Owner can maximize the value of the Product and the work of the Development Team

   a)   is clearly defined as a process in Scrum

   b)   may vary widely across organizations, Scrum Teams, and individuals

   c)   is not very different from traditional methods of Product Development

3.   A good practice of quality in Scrum is

   a)   Having dedicated quality assurance team

   b)   Verifying the quality at the Sprint boundaries

   c)   Building the quality into product from the beginning

4.   A general principle in Agile Product Development is

   a)   Build a lean version with crucial features and test the market before adding more features

   b)   Build a full version with all features and surprise the market with a perfect product

   c)   Aim to release some version to market at the end of first Sprint, no matter what

5.   Technical debt leads to

   a)   Products that are difficult to extend and maintain

   b)   Projects that are over-budget

   c)   Processes that lack tools

6.   To facilitate early releases, quality expectations can be reduced to save time

   a)   True

b) False

7. To verify the success of a product, what should be measured?

 a) ROI

 b) TCO

 c) Delivery of planned scope

 d) Customer Satisfaction

8. Revenue is the only measure of product's value

 a) Yes

 b) No

9. Product Owner needs to approve the definition of "Done"

 a) Yes

 b) Yes, but only when it is defined newly

 c) No

10. Product Owner can use these measures to track the true value being delivered

 a) Code Quality

 b) Customer Satisfaction

 c) Test Automation

 d) Cycle Time

11. When there are multiple Development Teams working on the same product

 a) they should collocate together and integrate their changes every day under the supervision of Scrum Master

b)   they should mutually define their definition of "Done" so their combined work will be potentially releasable

c)   they should ask the common quality guidance from the Product Owner

d)   they should define a definition of "Done" of their own, and make their standards transparent to each other

12.   What measures will help the Product Owner to check if the product delivers value?

a)   Total cost of the product throughout its life

b)   Productivity of Development Team

c)   The ease of absorption of new releases for the customers

d)   Customer Satisfaction

e)   On time completion of design

13.   Each Increment must be released to production to maximize the value

a)   True

b)   False

14.   To maximize the value, Product must order the Product Backlog based on the value of the Product Backlog Items

a)   True

b)   False

15.   By increasing the productivity of the Development Team, product's success can always be improved

a)   True

b)   False

Quiz - Answers

1.   Value is the measure of how valuable the delivered functionality is to the organization. It is a measure of the effectiveness (a percentage) of each dollar spent on software development that creates value for the organization. Prioritizing the investment on building highly usable features provide the highest chance of creating value. Correct answer is 'b'.

2.   Product Owner is responsible for maximizing the value of the Product and Developer Team work, by ensuring that the outcome have more ROI (Return on Investment) and less TCO (Total Cost of Ownership). But the specific process / method / techniques vary. Correct answer is 'b'.

3.   Building the quality into the Product from the beginning is a good practice, because it eliminates the potential of late rework and pushes the Product one step ahead towards the releasable quality. Correct answer is 'c'.

4.   Agile Manifesto recommends the principle 'Simplicity - The art of maximizing the amount of work not done.' Build only what is needed for user / customer to get most value and provide feedback on that. However, don't release an incomplete / bad quality product just to meet a time box. Correct answer is 'a'

5.   Technical debt refers to quality consequences by the poor technical choices made. Correct answer is 'a'.

6.   Every Increment must meet definition of "Done" thereby ensuring minimum quality standards. Quality goals cannot be reduced. Correct answer is 'b'.

7.   Just delivering the planned scope may not indicate a product success, unless it impacts the real value measures. Correct answers are 'a', 'b', and 'd'.

8.   Value is the measure of how valuable the delivered functionality is to the organization. Revenue is one measure of value but there are multiple notions of value, and it differs from organization to organization. Correct answer is 'b'.

9.   Development Team needs to follow any existing definition of "Done" defined by development organization. If nothing is available, Development Team must create one. The Product Owner's input should be considered, but no approval is necessary. Correct answer is 'c'.

10.   EBMgt Guide says "*Over the past two decades, many organizations have built software through the Scrum framework and the application of agile principles. Consequently, management efforts in software organizations often focus directly on the practices used rather than the outcomes produced. Managers in software organizations often seek to answer questions such as: "is build automation present?", "what is the quality of the code", "are developers integrating the code frequently", etc. While the answers to these questions may be interesting, unfortunately they are irrelevant to organizational value. Monitoring only the direct use of practices does not provide the best evidence of their effectiveness. For instance, tracking a Development Team's velocity is irrelevant to a Product Owner who is responsible for maximizing the value of the product.*" Correct answers are 'b' and 'd'.

11.   Each Development Team needs to mutually define their definition of "Done" so their combined work will be potentially releasable. Correct answer is 'b'.

12.   product cost ratio (TCO), Installed version index, usage index (amount of functionality being used), customer feedback are the direct measures of product value . Correct answers are 'a', 'c' and 'd'.

13.   Every Increment is of production quality so that there is transparency of work completion and prevention of technical debt. However, it is up to the Product Owner to choose to release to production. Sometimes it might be prudent for the Product Owner not to release from the standpoint that absorption of new release is not preferred by the customer (Installed Version Index). Correct answer is 'b'.

14.   It is not necessary to order based on the value of Product Backlog Items. Product Owner can consider many other parameters such as risk, dependencies between Product Backlog Items, even the dependencies to other products, etc such that the overall value of Development Team's work is optimized. Correct answer is 'b'.

15.   Team velocity and productivity are not direct measures of success of the product. Increase in productivity does not always mean the success of the product. Correct answer is 'b'.

##

Product Ownership in scaled Scrum

------------------------DE-TOUR------------------------

In this chapter, the following are included for clarity and context. They are not part of The Scrum Guide:

Nexus (Nexus is defined separately in Nexus Guide)

------------------------DE-TOUR------------------------

Large Teams and Scrum

Scrum.org provides a framework called Nexus, to scale the Scrum for large product development efforts. Since 5% of the questions are anticipated around large teams, you may want to familiarize with overall concepts in Nexus. Here is a summary of concepts in Nexus:

•   Nexus is a framework to integrate the work of approximately three to nine Scrum Teams working on a single product.

•   All Scrum Teams in a Nexus work from the same Product Backlog.

•   There is only one Product Owner in a Nexus.

•   All Scrum Teams in a Nexus together deliver one "Done" Integrated Increment at least every Sprint.

•   Nexus suggests team structuring to minimize the dependencies between different Scrum Teams. The dependency could be about common product requirements, distributed people with business and system knowledge, common code base, etc.

•   In addition to Scrum Teams, Nexus adds a new role called Nexus Integration Team. This is a team that consists of a Product Owner, a Scrum Master, and representative members from Scrum Teams.

•   Nexus Integration Team uses tools and practices to integrate the work and the product at larger scale. Such tools and practices may not be needed when only one Scrum Team works on a Product Backlog.

•   In addition to Daily Scrum within a Scrum Team, Nexus adds four new events: Nexus Sprint Planning, Nexus Daily Scrum, Nexus Review, and Nexus Retrospective. Sprint Review for individual Scrum Team is eliminated.

- In addition to common Product Backlog, Increment, and individual Sprint Backlog of each Scrum Team, Nexus requires two new artifacts. One is called Nexus Sprint Backlog. This is common Sprint Backlog for all Scrum Teams, and it is the composite of all Product Backlog Items from the Individual Sprint Backlogs. It is used to highlight dependencies and the flow of work during the Sprint. Another artifact is Nexus Sprint Goal which is the sum of individual Sprint Goals. Increment is called integrated Increment that represents the sum of all integrated work completed by a Nexus.

- Each item in the Product Backlog is continuously refined to a state called 'Thinly Sliced Functionality.'

- In Nexus Sprint Planning, appropriate team representatives from the Scrum Teams review the Product Backlog, and choose the items for their team. Within the Nexus Sprint Planning, each Scrum Team plans its Sprint, producing their Sprint Backlogs and Sprint Goals. The event ends with single Nexus Sprint Backlog and a Nexus Sprint Goal.

- In Nexus Daily Scrum, appropriate team representatives from the Development Teams discuss integration issues. Any relevant input is taken back to individual Daily Scrum of Development Teams.

- In Nexus Sprint Review, all Scrum Teams meet with Product Owner and key stakeholders to inspect the Increment and Product Backlog, and adapt the Product Backlog.

- In Nexus Sprint Retrospective, appropriate team representatives from the Scrum Teams identify issues common at Nexus level. Then, each Scrum Team conducts its Retrospective. Later, appropriate team representatives from the Scrum Teams bring the bottom up intelligence from Scrum Team retrospectives to visualize and track identified actions for common issues.

Product Owner and Product Backlog in Nexus

There is only one Product Owner in Nexus, and there is no separate Product Owner at individual Scrum Team level. Product is part of Nexus Integration Team. The responsibilities of the Product Owner are same as the responsibilities of typical Product Owner in Scrum.

Recollect that Nexus (framework for scaled Scrum) requires that the maximum number of Scrum Teams is limited to nine. If the Product requires larger team size than that, the product can be decomposed into separate products that are functionally and systematically separate. The decoupled products can have their own Product Owner.

Some of the merits of having only one Product Owner for each product are:

• There is transparency of who makes product decisions and priorities.

• Having the ultimate authority of decision with one person increases the speed of decisions.

During the Nexus Sprint Review, teams may not able to show all the work that was completed due to larger size of Increment. Product Owner should provide suggestions to prioritize what needs to be shown so that the feedback can be maximized.

During the Backlog Refinement and Nexus Sprint Planning, the Product Owner needs to let the team analyse the current Product Backlog and identify dependencies between teams. Product Owner should consider dependencies as another criterion to order the Product Backlog.

The frequency, duration, and extent of Backlog Refinement are expected to be little more intense than a single Scrum Team scenario. The levels of decomposition are likely to be more, and each item is refined until it is clear enough to be identified with a single Scrum Team. The dependency of the item on other Scrum Team is also captured. Refined Product Backlog should enable the visualization of which teams might deliver the items, and in what sequence over upcoming Sprints. The Product Backlog should be adequately refined with dependencies identified and removed or minimized prior to Nexus Sprint Planning.

Quiz - Questions

1. Identify the wrong implementations of Product Owner role

   a) Delegate Product Owner

   b) Proxy Product Owner

   c) Product Owner Committee

d) Co-located Product Owner

2. There are five Scrum Teams that are working on same product. How many Product Owners are needed?

a) As decided by the self-organized teams

b) Five Product Owners

c) Five Product Owners with Scrum Masters as backup

d) One Product Owner

3. What is the indication that the technical debt has become unacceptable?

a) when integration occurs, it remains unclear if all dependencies are resolved

b) when Daily Scrum occurs, the team members argue a lot

c) when Sprint Review occurs, the stakeholders provide a poor feedback

4. In a Nexus, each Scrum Team can end their Sprints at different dates

a) True

b) False

5. It is good practice to maintain separate Product Backlogs for multiple Scrum Teams that work on one product

a) True

b) False

6. When more Scrum Teams are added to a project that works on one single product, the productivity of the original Scrum Teams mostly likely will increase

a) True

b) False

Quiz – Answers

1.   Some implementations like Proxy Product Owner, Remote Product Owner, Product Owner Committee, etc increase miscommunication, slow-down in decision making, etc. A co-located Product Owner along with the Development Team is preferable. Correct answers are 'a', 'b' and 'c'.

2.   There is only one Product Owner for one product. Correct answer is 'd'.

3.   Software must be developed so that dependencies are detected and resolved before technical debt becomes unacceptable. The test of unacceptable technical debt is when integration occurs, and it remains unclear that all dependencies are resolved. In these cases, the unresolved dependencies remain hidden in the code and test base, lowering the overall value of the software. Correct answer is 'a'.

4.   Though it is not directly explained in Nexus Guide, we can see that Scrum Teams in a Nexus must sync their Sprint ends. Because, there is no individual Sprint Review and all the Scrum Teams need to have one common Nexus Sprint Review. After that all representatives of Scrum Teams need to participate in the Nexus Sprint Retrospective and end the Retrospective together. Correct answer is 'b'.

5.   There is only one Product Backlog for one product. Correct answer is 'b'.

6.   All Scrum Teams need to mutually define and adhere to their definition of "Done" so their combined work will be potentially releasable. This involves some overhead work in syncing up, and hence the negative impact to productivity. Correct answer is 'b'.

##

Other sources for preparation

There are many sites that offer free and paid mock questions for PSM 1 and PSPO 1 assessment. Again, beware of them. Many have misleading questions that will cloud your understanding of Scrum. It is better to steer clear of these sites.

The best mock exams are the Scrum Open and Product Owner Open offered by Scrum.org. Scrum Open contains 30 questions.

Product Owner Open contains 15 questions that resemble the original assessment format. It is available freely to anyone online:

Both Open assessments are available freely to anyone online: https://www.scrum.org/Assessments/Open-Assessments.

For each question, do not just stop with what was the right or best choice. Look at the other choices and clearly understand why they are not the best choices.

After attending open assessment, if you score more than 85% and you have good understanding of assessment.

Second time onwards, many of the same questions repeat. So, second time onwards, set a time limit of less than 10 minutes to complete the Scrum Open Assessment. DO NOT EVER RELAX THIS TIME. Because if you understood Scrum, you will reasonably think faster. Verify that you are able to score more than 90% within 10 minutes.

Have multiple attempts in open assessments until you get 100% in less than 10 minutes in a row.

Important: The open assessment questions are aimed at only testing the fundamental knowledge of Scrum and Product Owner role and hence are relatively easy compared to real assessment.

So, use the open assessment to understand the format and nuances in wording. For the real assessment, you need more preparation. Carefully practice all the questions provided in the book to practice locating right answer option, and understand why the other options are incorrect.

Books recommended by Scrum.org

Scrum.org lists additional sources to prepare for PSPO. The list contains around 13 books. Reading through all of them is a daunting task. Don't lose heart. In reality, you don't need to go through all of them.

Most of the books recommended by Scrum.org were published before the latest version of Scrum Guide 2016. As a result, there are lot inconsistent messages in them against the Scrum Guide.

As long as you have absorbed the content of Scrum Guide with its context and correlations, and thoroughly prepared using this book, you are mostly setup for the assessment.

##

Just before the exam

- Ensure that you had multiple attempts at the following open assessments in Scrum.org, until you get 100% in less than 10 minutes in a row.

Scrum Open Assessment

Product Owner Assessment

Nexus Open Assessment

- Have a final read at the 16 page Scrum Guide very slowly to digest each sentence. A good indication that you 'got' the Scrum Guide is - while you start reading the sentence, the gist of rest of the sentence will spontaneously pop in you head.

- Have a final read at the 10 page Nexus Guide very slowly to digest each sentence.

- Choose a convenient place to attend the assessment. Home is preferred since the organization's network may have firewall or usage restrictions.

- Ensure the place is well lit with no glare on the computer screen. The power supply should be uninterrupted. The internet connection is reliable with good speed in loading the screens in seconds.

- Remember that every minute is precious once you start the assessment. You can have a drink on the sides and face wipes to freshen up.

- Use Chrome or Firefox browser. Internet Explorer usually works fine too. However, Scrum.org cautions that certain version of Internet Explorer have been shown to be less reliable,

- Close all the unnecessary applications running on your computer including chat windows. If it helps, just have the softcopy of this book and the Scrum Guide open. You can quickly do any searches later during the review of bookmarked questions in the second pass.

- To attend the assessment, go to https://www.scrum.org/Assessments/Professional-Scrum-Product-Owner-Assessments.

- Click on hyperlink "Start PSPO I Now". It will prompt you to login. Login to Scrum.org account. If you haven't registered yet, please do so now.

- Enter the assessment password.

- You will be shown a page with technical considerations and quiz buttons. Read all the instructions.

- Once you click "Start this Assessment", the quiz is launched and clock starts ticking. There is a timer label at the top of the page, showing time remaining in minutes and seconds.

##

During the exam

- You will see the first question on the first page. First page has three buttons.

1 **Jump Back** - Clicking it takes to the first unanswered question.

2 **Submit->Forward** - This button with weird name, is the typical 'Next' button. You can click this to go to next question. You can answer the question and go to next. Without answering, you can also click the 'Bookmark this question' checkbox.

3 **Open Bookmarks** - Clicking this takes to a table containing the list of all the question numbers from 1 to 80. Any bookmarked question is shown with a tick mark.

- After answering first question, you can click Submit->Forward button to go to next page. Second page onwards has an additional button.

4 **Submit<-Back** - This button with weird name, is the typical 'Previous' button. You can click this to go back to previous question.

- On the last page, i.e., the page showing 80th question, you will see the following button instead of Submit->Forward.

5 **Save and Finish** - Clicking this button completes the test and submits it for assessment. Instead you can go back to previous question or open bookmarks to review any question.

- If you have prepared on the lines recommended in this book, you can complete answering all the questions in 35 - 45 minutes. Do not submit the test when you have more time. In the first pass, book mark the question that required second guessing. Later, use the additional time to review those questions.

- One very important note is- about the question that requires you to choose specific number of answers. Even if you fail to choose the required number of answers, the test won't prompt any error message. For example, if the question requires you to "choose two correct answers", and you checked only one checkbox for an answer and click "Submit->Forward" without checking one more checkbox, the test will simply move on. You will loose the points on that question.

##

Journey to Excellence is a Path. Good Luck on Your Journey!

###

Thank you for reading my book. Your one minute feedback means mountain of motivation to me. If you find it meeting your needs, and hopefully you have a minute to express that, could you leave a review at your favourite retailer?

Thanks!

Mohammed Musthafa Soukath Ali

About the Author

Mohammed Musthafa Soukath Ali

SCJP, LOMA 286, PMP, PSM, PSPO, SA, SPC

Musthafa is the author of the #1 Best Selling book Scrum Narrative and PSM Exam Guide in smashwords.com. He is ranked as one of the Tata Consultancy Services (TCS) Global Top Project Planners, acting as specialist coach for complex IT Application Development projects. He is also the external Management Capability Adviser for some of the Tata Group Companies. He is a designated Agile Software Delivery Expert, having consulted 10+ global customers. He published 9 papers in conferences with two international speaker invitations at Berlin/Spain. He is one of the Subject Matter Experts in TCS Corporate Agile Think-tank.

You can connect with the author through his linkedin network:

https://in.linkedin.com/in/mohammed-musthafa-soukath-ali-9a857762

##

Made in United States
Troutdale, OR
08/15/2023

12086350R00058